SKATEBOARDING

SKATEBOARDING

BY HOWARD REISER

FRANKLIN WATTS
NEW YORK •• LONDON
TORONTO •• SYDNEY
REVISED EDITION 1989
A VENTURE BOOK

Library of Congress Cataloging-in-Publicaton Data

Reiser, Howard.
Skateboarding / by Howard Reiser.—Rev. ed.
p.   cm.—(A Venture book)
Includes index.
Summary: Discusses choosing a skateboard, clothes and equipment
safety, injuries, how to skateboard, and stars in the field.
ISBN 0-531-10813-9
1. Skateboarding—Juvenile literature.   2. Skateboarding.
I. Title.
GV859.8.R44   1989
796.2′1—dc20   89-32406   CIP   AC

Originally published as *Skateboarding* (A First Book)
Second Edition
Copyright © 1978, 1989 by Howard Reiser
Printed in the United States of America
5   4   3   2

TO MY FAMILY

The author would like to thank:

Ralph Cipriani, Jr., Boulevard Riding Systems
Limited in Garden City Park, New York;
J.T. Murphy; Russ Howell; and the National
Skateboard Association.

Photographs courtesy of:

Robert A.M. Boswell: pp. 2, 10, 15, 41, 87 (top);
Mark Zemnick: pp. 13, 44, 50, 53, 54, 60,
65, 70; Photo Researchers: pp. 30 (Robert A.
Isaacs), 38 (Barbara Rios), 57 (Herman Emmet),
62 (Robert A. Isaacs), 67 and 68 (Bruce Roberts);
Randy Matesow: pp. 39, 47; Gamma-Liaison:
p. 73 (E. Sander); Eastern Skateboarding
Association: pp. 84, 87 (bottom), 90.

CONTENTS

······································

SKATEBOARDING

MODERN SKATEBOARDING

. . . .

The boy took a deep breath. He looked straight ahead, making certain that no one was in his path. Then he began to ride down the steep, curved hill, the wheels of his skateboard tightly gripping the pavement. His slim body was bent low, his long arms extended. His eyes were wide with excitement.

This boy, and many youngsters like him, is taking to the pavement in a sport that has boomed practically overnight. Millions of people participate. Large skateboarding competitions are held in big arenas with

Many young people have become avid participants in the popular sport of skateboarding.

skateboarders competing for large sums of prize money. And most experts agree: Skateboarding is here to stay.

SURFERS DISCOVER
SOMETHING NEW

Though it began to gain real attention in the early 1970s, skateboarding first became popular in southern California ten years earlier. When the boards were first introduced, surfers grabbed them. They saw at once that the same skills they used in surfing could also be used in skateboarding. Thus, for them, skateboarding became something they could do when surfing was not possible.

By 1965, up to 50 million skateboards had been sold in the United States. They were being bought almost as quickly as they could be made, and not just by surfers. But by the end of that year, it was becoming apparent that interest in the sport was rapidly declining. Skateboarding was disappearing from the scene. What had happened?

THE SKATEBOARD
DISAPPEARS . . .
AND THEN REAPPEARS

Many reasons have been offered as to why interest in skateboarding nearly died. But probably the single most important factor was the poor quality of the skateboard itself, especially the wheels, which made

New manufacturing techniques have yielded skateboards that allow riders increased freedom.

the sport dangerous and expensive. Because of its manufacturing limitations, the skateboard could not provide the rider with exciting new ways to use it. Even a simple routine could cause the rider to fall off the board. And the boards themselves would often break apart under only minor impacts. Thus, many people became bored or discouraged with the sport.

For nearly ten years the skateboard's popularity continued to decline. But in 1973, improved skateboards were introduced on the market. Not only could a person do more things on the modern board, but the ride was much safer, too. It wasn't long before the new boards were being produced by a variety of companies in California and on the East Coast. Skateboard sales jumped. Large orders for boards started coming in from foreign countries. Magazines such as *Skateboarder* and *Skateboard* sprang up and helped to further interest in the sport. (These magazines have now been replaced by others such as: *Transworld Skateboarding*, *Thrasher*, and *Power-edge*.) By 1975, skateboarding was back on the scene, bigger and more popular than ever.

THE MODERN SKATEBOARD

The person most responsible for the current popularity of skateboarding was Frank Nasworthy, a California surfer. In 1973, Nasworthy came up with the idea of replacing the baked clay wheels with urethane plastic ones. Soon after boards with these new wheels appeared, interest in the sport began to zoom.

deck

truck

bearing

wheel

kicktail

THE WHEELS

The main advantage of the new urethane wheels was their outstanding gripping surface. Because of them, the board could better absorb the shock of rolling over pebbles and other tiny objects, thus lessening the chance that the rider would fall head over heels, a position he or she often ended up in when the old clay wheels were used. The urethane wheels also allowed the rider to execute safe, sharp turns. And, in addition, the urethane wheels lasted much longer.

Urethane wheels nowadays are made two basic ways: by a pour-molding process and by an injection-molding process. Most skaters prefer wheels made by the pour-molding method. To make sure you are getting pour-molded wheels when you buy a skateboard, check for flat spots or blemishes on the edges. If there are any, the wheels were probably injection molded. Injection-molded wheels also do not spin as well, and thus give the rider an uneven, wobbly ride. Largely for these reasons, the injection-molding process is not used much anymore.

WHEEL
INSPECTION

It is very important that your skateboard wheels be perfect when you buy it. Never buy a skateboard without first carefully inspecting the wheels. To make certain the wheels are in good condition:

•• Make sure there are no flat spots on their surfaces.

•• Spin the wheels; if they wobble or come to an abrupt stop, don't buy the board.

•• Make certain there are no manufacturing defects, such as markings on the wheels.

•• The wheels should provide good traction (gripping ability) and stability, as well as speed and durability. To test for these qualities, first run the skateboard along a smooth surface to get the feel of how it grips the surface. Then gently push your fingernail into each wheel. It should sink in just a little. Finally, press down on the wheels with your thumb. You shouldn't be able to make a depression in the surface.

DETERMINING
THE RIGHT WHEEL
SIZE FOR YOU

You should consider what kind of skateboarding you will be doing before choosing skateboard wheels and decks. Different types of skateboarding require different kinds of equipment. You should read chapter 3 before you buy a skateboard. And keep in mind that even if you are just a beginner, you will probably soon want to try out new things on your skateboard other than basic riding.

Skateboard wheels come in two basic varieties:

•• *Standard wheels:* These are about 1⅛ inches (2.9 cm) wide (wheel thickness) by 1½ inches (3.8 cm) in diameter. These wheels are popular among those doing basic freestyle tricks. But they do not grip the pavement well when going at a fast speed. There-fore, it would not be a good idea to use these wheels for speed or slalom riding, or even for any of the more fancy freestyle maneuvers. However, these wheels are popular among beginners learning to do routine skateboarding tricks.

•• *Extra-large wheels:* These are about 2¼ inches (5.8 cm) wide by 2⅝ inches (6.7 cm) in diameter. The extra-large wheels permit the experienced skater to enjoy both a fast and stable ride. Therefore, it is not surprising that most of those who ride these wheels concentrate on downhill speed riding. Be-cause the board is high off the ground, it is difficult to do freestyle tricks on wheels this size. Skaters should first get experience riding the smaller wheels before trying out the bigger ones.

BEARINGS

Tiny, precision steel balls are contained inside each skateboard wheel. These steel balls are called bear-ings. Bearings permit the wheel to spin freely, thus enabling the rider to enjoy a smooth ride. Skateboard wheels contain two major types of bearings: sealed precision ball bearings and loose (or open) ball bear-ings self-contained in the wheel.

Sealed precision ball bearings are fairly new to skateboard wheels. However, they are considered the best of the two because:

•• They provide a smooth, fast, steady, and quiet ride.

- • The wheel will not wobble, even at high speeds.
- • No personal maintenance is required.

Though precision ball bearings are expensive, in the long run they will probably prove to be economical. Be sure you buy what are called *double-sealed* ball bearings. These will hold up better than single-sealed ones.

Loose ball bearings self-contained in the wheel are not as popular as the sealed precision ball bearings. Although the self-contained loose ball bearing wheel is inexpensive, it does not provide as good a ride as the sealed precision ball bearing wheel.

A skateboard also consists of two other main parts: the deck, also called the board, and the trucks, which are the metal suspension systems on which the wheels are mounted.

THE DECKS

The original decks, or boards, on skateboards consisted mainly of hard, solid wood. But in the 1970s, skaters had the advantage of being able to ride on a variety of more flexible materials (flexboards). Thus, skaters using these boards could do many more exciting skating routines.

However, during the 1980s, a new type of wooden deck became most popular among skateboarders. Composed of several layers, the board is both sturdy and lightweight and has the much sought-after flexing capability. It also absorbs vibrations extremely well, does not often splinter, and is easily shaped by manufacturers for functional use.

While the original, solid wooden boards were primarily used for downhill racing and gymnastic maneuvers, the newer and lighter boards serve all types of skaters. The decks are generally made of the highest quality wood—oak, maple, or beech—with the grain running both the length and width of the board. When you buy a wooden skateboard, also purchase inexpensive non-slip grip tape. Lay a few strips of the tape down the length of your board. This will help you achieve better riding balance and will reduce the chances of your slipping and hurting yourself.

FLEXBOARDS

In the 1970s and early 1980s, flexboards were heavily used by skaters. The boards absorbed shock very well when riding over rough spots and could easily be made to go faster, slower, or make sharp turns by using the weighting or unweighting process. By weighting (pressing down hard on the board), a skater could ride faster and make sharp turns. A board slows down when the skater unweights (reduces pressure on the board). Although flexboards were easily controlled by the skater through the weighting and unweighting procedure, they were largely replaced in the mid-1980s by the modern wooden board.

During the skateboarding boom of the 1970s, the most popular flexboard materials were plastic, fiberglass, and aluminum. Although plastic boards continue to be used, they are primarily restricted to skaters wishing to learn basic maneuvers. Plastic boards are also relatively inexpensive—the average cost of the boards is usually under $30. However, the disadvantages of riding the plastic boards are that they may sag under stress; may become soft if left out in the sun for an extended period of time; may become brittle and crack if exposed to cold weather; and are not strong enough to permit grabrails and other accessories to be attached.

Fiberglass boards were originally very popular, largely because they had good flexibility and were very sturdy. However, skaters in the 1980s discovered that the fiberglass boards did not provide as smooth a ride as the wooden boards; were too heavy and unwieldy and were easily damaged; and, like the plastic boards, the fiberglass material could not accommodate functional accessories.

Although aluminum boards were attractive and flexible, they were expensive and, in many instances, unsafe. As a result of constant scraping against the curb and pavement, the edges and tips of the boards often became dangerously sharp. This caused much concern among riders. The flexing ability of the aluminum product suddenly did not seem important once the modern wooden skateboard came into use.

KICKTAILS

Virtually all skateboards have kicktails. Kicktails come in a variety of shapes and angles, offering riders a range of choices depending upon personal preference. In general, because of comfort and safety, the gradual kicktail is preferred to the one that turns up sharply. But some skaters who use the sharp kicktail claim it serves to hook their back foot in place while doing maneuvers.

As contrasted to the earlier, non-kicktail flat boards, kicktails enable the rider to more easily lift the nose of the board off the ground and do more freestyle tricks. Further, the skater's back foot is provided with a snug resting place, so that it does not slide off the back of the board as easily as it would on a flat board. Many boards even have kicknoses, which may help in doing certain tricks. When you buy a board, you should first make certain that the kicktail provides a comfortable resting place for your rear foot. After all, if you are not comfortable riding a board, you won't enjoy the ride. And the chances of your getting hurt will be increased.

DECK SIZES

There are three basic skateboard lengths, each of which is widely used:

•• 24 inches (61 cm). Known as a "mini" board, its popularity has zoomed recently. It is primarily used by skaters who are not very big or who have small-size feet. Those riding this board find it much easier to maneuver than the larger decks. Consequently, they enjoy a more exciting and safer ride.

•• Another 24-inch (61-cm) size board (not the "mini"), considered almost in the "toy" category, is used by many beginners. Primarily made of plastic materials, its inexpensive cost of up to $30 makes this board practical for learners. But when a skater improves his or her riding skills, he or she will generally no longer use this small-sized board.

•• 27 inches (67 cm). Largely used for freestyle maneuvers, this board is generally made of wooden material with limited flexing capacity. The board—very popular with skateboard gymnasts—usually contains a very small kicktail.

•• 29 to 32 inches (74 to 82 cm). These are heavily used for street riding, ramp riding, and a host of streetstyle maneuvers. Made of wooden material, the boards normally contain physical characteristics that enable skaters to do tricks more easily. In addition to their greater length, the boards are between 9 and 11 inches (23 and 28 cm) in width—at least several inches wider than other deck sizes. The large overall size of the boards provides skaters with sturdier and smoother rides. However, because of their large size, the boards are sometimes difficult to maneuver. Therefore, they should be mainly used by experienced skaters who feel comfortable riding the large boards.

Many skateboarders make the mistake of choosing a board solely on the basis of how tall or how heavy they are. Instead, you should buy the board size that best fits your skating needs.

TRUCKS

The metal suspension systems on which the wheels are mounted are called the trucks. Shock pads are built into these trucks to absorb jolts. A good quality truck part will not only help you enjoy a smoother ride, but will also help you make better and quicker turns. You should make sure that the trucks on your board are evenly placed. Otherwise, the skateboard will not ride straight, and the wheels will wear out quicker than they should.

You should also consider how the trucks are mounted. If they are attached close to the tips of the board, you will have a *long* wheelbase. A shorter wheelbase is made by having the trucks placed further from the ends of the board. You should have your trucks mounted according to the type of riding you wish to do. Short wheelbases are especially good for doing wheelies, kickturns, and other freestyle maneuvers (see chapter 3). A longer wheelbase—preferred by downhill speedsters—provides better balance for the high-speed rider. And skaters looking for greater flexibility in their boards would be more apt to find it in a board with a long wheelbase rather than a short one.

SKATEBOARD
ACCESSORIES

Skateboard accessories, also known as "add ons," first became an important feature of skateboards in the late 1970s. These additional items serve to either better protect the board from damage or to enable the skater to better perform a variety of maneuvers. The accessories include:

•• *Grabrails.* Approximately 1-foot (⅓-meter) long plastic rods, they are attached lengthwise at left and right sides to the bottom of the board. The rails serve as handles for various stunts and also make the board stronger and more durable.

•• *Tailplates.* Placed across the width of the bottom of the kicktail, they protect the board from being damaged during maneuvers. Consequently, the plates help the board to last longer and to save costs.

•• *Nose guard.* Urethane or rubber bumper placed across the nose of the board, it protects the nose from damage.

•• *Lapper* or *curb hopper.* This is attached to the front or the rear skateboard truck. Serving as a sort of miniature ramp, it helps riders to skate over curbs and other inclines.

•• *Coper.* A plastic device that fits atop the front and rear truck axles, it contributes to a smoother skateboard ride and protects the trucks from wear and tear.

KEEPING
YOUR EQUIPMENT
IN SHAPE

There is nothing more important in skateboarding than making certain that your board is always kept in good working order. Your failure to properly maintain your piece of riding equipment will certainly prevent you from enjoying good rides. Also, it could easily cause you to have a serious riding accident. Finally, a skateboard that is neglected will not last very long.

You will wind up having to make constant and costly repairs or being forced to buy a new piece of equipment altogether. In the long run, you will save money and time if you take care of your skateboard.

THE WHEELS

In maintaining your board, one of the first things you must do is always make sure that your wheels are turning easily. After all, you can't enjoy your rides if your wheels are not rotating as they should be.

BEARING TROUBLE

Some of the reasons wheels don't turn properly are a result of bearing trouble. Perhaps you have:

•• Dirty bearings. Make certain the bearings are kept clean. Use "bearing spray," sold in skateboard and sporting goods stores, to remove dust and dirt that can collect.

•• A "too tight" outside bearing race nut in the wheels. Loosen the bearing nut to achieve a better wheel spin.

WOBBLY WHEELS

Wheels that wobble are also dangerous to the rider. Very often, skateboarders do not pay attention to "wheel wobble" until after they have been thrown off their boards. Always carry a skatekey with you while skating. This way you can make certain the truck bolt is sufficiently tightened so as to prevent any wheel wobble. The bolt should be tightened so that there is *some* pressure between the bolt and the truck plate.

A CROOKED ROLL

Before you ride on your skateboard, place it on flat ground and give it a slight push to see if it rolls in a straight line. If the board veers off to the side, you will know that there is something wrong. Your board might require a truck adjustment or have an axle or bolt that has been bent out of shape. In most cases, the best thing to do is to bring the skateboard to a shop, where the equipment can be professionally checked out.

REPLACING PARTS

Wheels and bearings generally wear out quicker than other parts of the skateboard. However, it is difficult to predict how often these parts will have to be replaced. Usually, the condition of the wheels and bearings depends upon how much riding you do. To help you get the best possible wheel performance— and to prevent the wheels from wearing down unevenly—you should rotate your wheels every four or five weeks, from front left to rear right, front right to left rear, rear left to front right, and rear right to front left.

DECKS

Wooden decks normally will not suffer any cracks. These boards are extremely sturdy. However, riders should always make it a point to check for signs of cracks in their decks. A skater noticing deep cracks down the middle of his or her board should bring the board into a skateboard shop for inspection and possible repairs or replacement. A board that has significant cracks should not be ridden.

PLAYING
IT SAFE

If you enjoy skateboarding but refuse to pay attention to safety practices, you can be sure that, sooner or later, you will hurt yourself badly. Not only will you suffer painful injuries, but other skateboarders or innocent bystanders could also get hurt as a result of your disregard for safety rules. Therefore, for your own well-being—and for the well-being of others—it is important that you be a safety-conscious, responsible skateboarder.

PROPER
CLOTHES AND
EQUIPMENT

To cut down on the chances of hurting yourself while skateboarding, you should always wear the proper clothes—long pants (blue jeans are best) and a long-sleeve shirt. These serve as basic protection against cuts and bruises from falls—and you will fall. (See the section on learning to fall properly, in chapter 2.)

Be sure to wear rubber-soled or athletic shoes that do not have any heels. If the heel of your shoe were to jab you during a fall, you could be badly hurt.

Also, the rubber soles grip the surface of the board better. Always be sure when you start your ride that your laces are tightly tied. *Under no conditions should you skate barefoot.* Even under normal circumstances, your feet will probably suffer a variety of minor scrapes and cuts. Don't make it harder on your feet.

As in other sports, certain equipment should be worn to protect you from injuries common to the sport. Heavy garden-type gloves and knee and elbow pads are a must. Unfortunately, many skateboarders fail to wear them. And since so many skateboard accidents involve head injuries, helmets should also be worn, particularly by downhill speed racers.

At this time, not too many helmets are being made strictly for skateboarding. However, you can't go wrong buying the same type of helmet worn by bicycle riders. They are of an open-type construction, lightweight, and flexible. A good helmet need not be expensive. If you still think it is too much trouble to bother with a helmet, limit yourself to the most basic type of skateboard cruising, or you may wind up in a hospital.

WHERE TO GO
SKATEBOARDING
SAFELY

Picking out a place to go skateboarding is simple. You can have a lot of fun in your own driveway, or, perhaps, on a quiet, dead-end street near your home. Even a schoolyard or playground is good—anywhere there is a smooth *traffic-free* patch of pavement.

At a specially designed skateboard park
in California, this safety-conscious skater
wears gloves, elbow and knee pads, a helmet,
and rubber-soled shoes to avoid injury.

As a beginner, choose a flat area, such as an empty parking lot. If there are other skateboarders around, spend some time watching them before you start. But remember: Don't try to perform the stunts or routines you see experienced skateboarders do.

Even though skateboarding has grown quite popular since the early 1970s, there are still few areas set aside for skateboarding only. As of now, only a handful of skateboarding parks are in use throughout the country. In time, as the sport gains more fans, it is hoped that more parks will be developed.

The parks that are now open offer riders the chance to skate on ramps, flat surfaces, slopes, and other types of grounds and surfaces. There, skateboarders also have the advantage of being in the company of advanced skaters, people whom they can observe and learn a lot from. Those who go to these parks are also skating under much safer conditions than those who skateboard in the street. Naturally, they do not have traffic to watch out for. And also, skaters at these parks are required to wear the proper clothing and are observed by park supervisors.

CAMPS

The continued popularity of skateboarding during the 1980s has led to the opening of summer skateboard camps. Youngsters attending these camps are virtually assured of improving their riding skills under the supervision of top professional and amateur skaters. In addition, campers also often make new friends from among other young skaters.

Although each camp is run differently, most camp programs range from between three and six weeks.

Campers generally sign up for at least one week of participation. Along with the intensive skating instruction, food and sleep-over accommodations are also provided.

Those wishing to obtain information about skateboard camps should contact an appropriate skateboard association, or speak to skaters who have attended camps or who know of others who have. Although most camps are well run, a prospective camper should first find out everything he or she can about a camp before making a commitment to attend.

SOME BASIC
SAFETY RULES

Here are some safety tips you should always follow. If you do, you will greatly decrease the chances of getting hurt:

• • Never show off.
• • Don't cross intersections while riding your skateboard. Instead, carry your board across the street.
• • Never ride blindly into a street from behind a parked car.
• • Loosen the main skateboard nut a half-turn with a skatekey and the main bolt a turn-and-a-half (both counterclockwise) if your board tilts upward on turns.
• • When you are just starting out, the main bolt should be snug against the rubber cushions on the truck, for the most stable ride.

•• Never ride on wet pavement, through a puddle, over pebbles, or on sand. Urethane wheels won't grip on wet surfaces and may get ruined if water or sand gets inside.
•• Learn to fall properly (see chapter 2).
•• Don't try riding on a terrain that appears too difficult, especially for downhill racing.

COMMON SKATE-
BOARD INJURIES

Although most skateboard injuries involve only minor scrapes and bruises, skateboarders do occasionally suffer fractures and other more serious injuries. Skateboarders trying to reduce the impact of their falls with their hands often wind up breaking their arms or wrists.

And serious elbow injuries have become so common to the sport that doctors refer to a particular type of injury as "skateboard elbow." Head, shoulder, knee, and ankle injuries caused by falls also frequently occur, and, just as in other sports, some accidents have even resulted in death.

While skateboard-related injuries have jumped dramatically in recent years, there is little doubt that most serious accidents could have been easily avoided if the skaters had worn the proper clothes and equipment and observed other safety tips. Certainly, skateboarders will always fall sometimes. But the safety measures they can take will prevent many of the painful and serious injuries now unnecessarily experienced.

WHAT YOU CAN
DO ABOUT INJURIES

It is very important that you know what first-aid steps to take if you or someone else were to get hurt while skateboarding. Whether the injury involves heavy bleeding, bone fractures, or other types of severe wounds, quick action on your part could prevent tragedy.

BLEEDING

If someone is bleeding badly, don't waste any time before acting, since it is possible to bleed to death *in one minute* if a large blood vessel has been severed. Take any clean cloth, roll it up into a pad, and press it down onto the wound. Your object is to stop or control the bleeding until a doctor or other professional help arrives.

FRACTURES

Very often, a person who has just suffered a fractured (broken) bone does not experience much pain if the injured portion of the body is not moved. Because of this, it could be difficult to determine whether the accident victim has, in fact, broken a bone. Clues indicating that a fracture has resulted are:

•• The victim will likely experience pain if someone applies pressure by pressing down on the skin over the injured portion of the body.
•• There will be a swelling in the area of the fracture.

•• *34*

A person who has suffered an apparent fracture should *not* be moved until the fractured bone is made immobile. If help can reach you, just wait for it. But, if in an emergency you have to make your own splint, you can use a sturdy piece of cardboard, a pillow, a newspaper, a piece of wood, or any flat substance. Cloth padding should be placed between the skin and the splint.

DON'T MOVE
  SOMEONE WHO IS
SERIOUSLY INJURED

If someone is seriously injured, it is best not to move the person at all. Summon medical help. Moving a badly injured person could make the injuries more serious or even cause the patient to lapse into a condition known as shock. If in an emergency it is necessary to move the person, you should carry him or her in such a way as to best prevent the injury from becoming worse. More detailed instructions can be found in a first-aid booklet in your school library or by contacting organizations such as the Red Cross or the Boy Scouts.

TWO

SO YOU WANT
TO LEARN

As a beginner, you would do well to buy an inexpensive skateboard. But be sure to get one with good flexibility and urethane wheels. Buy your skateboard in a skateboard store if your town has one, or from a surf and ski shop, bicycle shop, or sporting goods store. Department stores and many toy stores also handle skateboard equipment, but try not to buy your board there. Very often these stores do not have a good selection, nor do the salespeople often have a thorough knowledge about what they are selling.

DO YOU
NEED LESSONS?

Most young people learn to skateboard by themselves or with a group of friends. But it might be wise to try and take some lessons, especially if you are serious about your skateboarding. Find out whether anyone in your area gives formal lessons by contacting your local parks or recreation department, or local skateboard or surf shop. At the very least, you will be told where in your community skateboarders go. A visit to a skateboard area might result in finding someone who can teach you. You might also call your local ice- or roller-skating rink for information.

YOU'RE
READY TO START

Place one foot on top of the board and gently push off with the other. Pedal around slowly and patiently, until you get the feel of it. When you feel sure of yourself, place your second foot on top of the board after the push-off and coast a little.

Learning how to get both feet on the board properly is very important. If your feet are planted too close together or too far apart, you'll feel uncomfortable for the whole ride. Although the most basic riding stance for skateboard cruising is placing the left foot pointing forward slightly across the width of the rear portion of the board, the important thing is for *you* to feel comfortable while you are riding. Placing your feet parallel across the width of the board may feel more balanced to you. In time, you may alter your riding stance. But when you are first learning, it is most important that you be relaxed and feel in control of the board. To attain good balance, try keeping your hands and arms a little out in front of you and your knees slightly bent. And always look straight ahead, never downward or sideways.

Left: standing on your skateboard may feel a bit awkward at first. Take some time to get used to your board.
Above: the skater on the left holds his arms out for balance, while the girl on the right prepares to skate away.

LEARNING
TO FALL

If you are going to skateboard a lot, you should expect to fall at least once in a while. All professional athletes, especially skiers and ice skaters, take a fall when they are experimenting with new moves. Therefore, you should learn to fall the *correct* way. That way you will reduce the chances of hurting yourself when you do fall.

First, always remember that the closer your body is to the ground when you fall, the less chance you will have of getting hurt. When you feel yourself about to fall (and you *do* always know just a little ahead of it), lower your body closer to the ground, stay calm, and try rolling off your board. You can much more easily break a bone or injure yourself badly if all your weight comes down on one portion of your body, such as a wrist or elbow.

When you feel yourself falling, protect your face and head by throwing an arm across the eye area. Also, you should practice falling on a grassy lawn before you start serious skateboarding.

When you feel yourself falling, fight the urge to throw out your arms as the rider to the right has done. Instead, lower your body and try to roll off your board.

LEARNING
TO TURN

Once you have become used to riding your board, you will probably want to learn how to make good turns. Turns are made for stopping, slowing down, speeding up, controlling your board while heading downhill, and for most tricks and stunts.

Your ability to turn will most likely determine whether you will become a good skateboarder or not. And, if you do not take the time to learn how to turn properly, you will not only be missing out on a lot of fun, but, even more importantly, you will not be skateboarding safely.

Before you make your first turn, check that your feet are well balanced on your board and that you are completely comfortable. There is no set rule on how far apart your feet should be. Many new riders feel most comfortable with their feet about 12 inches (30 cm) apart. Later, after much practice and trying out different positions, you will develop your own riding stance.

To turn, twist your body in the direction you want to go. If you wish to make a right turn, lean your body to the right; if you want to go left, lean your body to the left. The further you lean in the direction of the turn, the sharper your turn will be. Look in the direction you want to turn, then quickly rotate your shoulders and hips in that direction. The rotation will cause the board to change directions. Never jerk your body at the last moment to make a sudden turn. A quick movement could easily cause a fall. Plan your turns. And remember to lean into your turns *before* the board has completely turned (forward and to the side). Don't twist your body at all.

When you wish to stop the turn and resume riding in a straight direction, shift the weight of your body back toward the middle of the board, first rotating your hips and then your shoulders.

Many skateboarders find that by lowering their bodies closer to the ground while they ride, they can turn easier. If you want to learn how to do this, try it on a slightly sloped pavement and be prepared to spend a lot of time doing it. Once you have mastered this style of riding, you will probably find turning more exciting and enjoyable.

In the beginning, you will no doubt find turning a little difficult to do. But like other things, the more you practice, the better you will become. Even if you choose to do nothing more than basic slow-riding skateboarding, turning is something you should take the time to learn, just as you took the time to learn how to make turns on your bicycle.

STOPPING
THE BOARD

A beginning skateboarder not knowing how to stop his or her board can easily get hurt. One basic way to stop or get off a board is to first slow it down and then get off, first with the back foot and then with the front foot. Completing a turn so that the board points upward on a hilly pavement or dragging the rear tip of the board against the ground after doing freestyle movements are two other good ways of stopping the board.

LAWS RESTRICTING
SKATEBOARDING ACTIVITY

As a result of complaints from many non-skateboard-
ers and motorists, some places have established laws
restricting skateboarding activity. Some local govern-
ments have prohibited skateboarders from riding on
busy streets. And some reckless skateboarders have
been given summonses by police for endangering
themselves and others.

To find out whether there are any laws restricting
skateboarding in your area, contact your local city hall,
parks department, or local police for information. And
obey the laws. They protect you and make skateboarding safer for everyone.

Be a responsible skater.
Obey all local laws
and warning signs.

THREE

....

POPULAR TRICKS
AND ROUTINES

One of the reasons skateboarding has become more and more popular is because skaters can do so many different stunts and routines. You might not be very good at, or enjoy doing, certain tricks. But there are so many to choose from, it hardly matters. And this applies to beginners as well as to more advanced skaters. Perhaps you will want to become great at doing wheelies. Your friend might find spins and turns more exciting. Some advanced skaters like riding up the walls of empty pools, in drainage ditches, and around reservoirs; others love to do gymnastic tricks on skateboards. There are skateboarders who like to jump over high bars or over barrels. Skaters who have had previous ballet training can often be seen doing their ballet routines on their boards. And as you become more skilled, you might even make up some new skating routines, ones that others will want to imitate. Let's look now at how some of these tricks are done.

*Skateboarder executing advanced move
in New York City's Washington Square Park*

FREESTYLE
SKATEBOARDING

Many of the popular tricks in skateboarding fall within the freestyle category. Freestyle tricks can be performed almost anywhere there is some unused space. After you become good at doing a number of them, you can put some together to create a routine, much like the routines done by figure skaters. Here are some of the favorite freestyle stunts:

THE WHEELIES

This is one of the basic movements done by skateboarders. It can be learned without too much practice. Dramatic looking, wheelie movements usually act as a starting point for other tricks.

Basically, all wheelies involve placing one or both feet at one end of the board, causing the wheels on the other end to raise up off the ground. The variations of this trick include:

•• *One-foot nose wheelies.* Riding with one foot placed on the front end of the board, causing the back wheels to rise off the ground.

•• *Two-foot nose wheelies.* Riding with both feet on the front end of the board, causing the rear wheels to rise off the ground.

•• *Squat-nose wheelie.* The toughest of nose-wheelie variations. Starting in standing position, crouch to squat position, then stand up again—a difficult balancing act.

•• *One-foot tail wheelies*. Riding with one foot on the back end of the board, causing the front wheels to rise off the ground.

•• *Two-foot tail wheelies*. Riding with both feet on the rear end of the board, causing the front wheels to rise off the ground.

•• *Two-board wheelies*. Riding with one foot placed on the front end of the board, the other foot placed on the rear end of another board, causing two of the wheels from each board to rise off the ground.

•• *Handstand wheelies*. Using the hands (by being in a handstand position on the board) to get the front or back wheels of the board off the ground.

Although skaters have different ways of placing their feet on the board while doing wheelies, it is most important to keep the body weight balanced over the wheels that are riding along the pavement. Tail wheelies are generally much easier to do than nose wheelies. This is because it is easier to get your weight balanced over the rear of the board than over the front.

KICKTURNS

Another basic skateboarding trick, kickturns, too, are fairly simple to learn. Skateboarders who have learned how to do kickturns often become better at doing wheelie tricks, 360s, and other riding routines.

To do kickturns, you put one foot on the rear of the board and the other foot toward the front. While the back foot pushes down on the tail, the nose lifts

off the ground, and the front foot directs the board from side to side. In between turns, the front wheels quickly strike the pavement.

Pretty to watch, kickturners control their boards well along flat surfaces at surprisingly fast speeds and often race against each other. This stunt is a popular one in organized skateboarding contests.

360s

This is one of the most flashy skateboarding tricks. It is, simply, making a complete spinning rotation, with either the front or back wheels off the ground. 360s can be done in various ways, such as by spinning clockwise or counterclockwise, or using one or two feet. Many riders continue their 360 spins as long as they can without stopping.

This trick requires skill, perfect timing, and good balance. Anyone who has learned to do 360s probably will have already learned how to do wheelies, kickturns, and other turning maneuvers. But even if you never learn to do 360s well, you will become more familiar with the feel of your board by trying to learn this stunt.

OLLIE

This is one of the most popular stunts among both experienced skaters and those who have already mastered basic skateboarding maneuvers. To do this,

One-foot tail wheelie

you press your rear foot on the tail of the board, causing the front of the board to lift up. Then you slide your front foot from the middle of the board to the front, enabling the board to momentarily rise off the ground.

Skateboarders perform this stunt to jump over objects placed on the ground or to maneuver the board to rise over street curbs or other elevations. Since it requires good balance, the trick should not be attempted by skaters who have not first learned basic skateboarding skills, or do not yet feel totally comfortable with their board.

FINGERFLIP

Although skaters have fun performing this trick, it should not be attempted by an inexperienced rider, or one who is not agile. Basically, you place both feet on the tail of the board, causing the rear wheels to touch the ground. Then, crouching low, you flip the nose of the board over and, at virtually the same moment, jump into the air. Then you land on the board with both feet.

After completing the stunt, some skaters immediately begin a series of other maneuvers without first getting off the board. Most do not. The important thing is that skaters should not be careless when doing the stunt. Otherwise, they can easily break an ankle or suffer another type of injury.

Skater performing an ollie
*from a skating bank onto
a street ramp*

THE CATAMARAN

This trick is done with two people. The skaters sit across the width of their boards, grab each other's hands, hook their feet together, and head down a hill together, sideways.

Half the fun of the catamaran is trying to get the boards to head in the right direction. The other half, it seems, is when the skaters roll off their boards in a tangle together somewhere along the way. Although this stunt can be a lot of fun, don't do it going down a steep hill or without wearing protective equipment. Also make sure you are not heading in the direction of a busy roadway.

JUMPING

Skateboard jumping tricks offer the excitement and "free" feeling many advanced skateboarders look for. These tricks require proper timing, good coordination, and perfect balance to do. You shouldn't try them until you feel quite at home on your skateboard. Among the most popular jumping tricks are:

•• *Board-to-board jumping.* This is probably the first jumping stunt you should attempt. This trick requires good balance and deep concentration, but not the skill you will need for other routines such as barrel and high jumping. Board-to-board jumping is done by riding one board toward another board that has been placed on the ground ahead. You prepare for the jump

Fingerflip

by crouching as you approach the second board. When you jump, try to land in the middle of the second board, with both feet evenly balanced. After landing, quickly move your feet into your normal skateboard riding position. If you feel you have not had a good start, do not try to complete the jump. It is much safer to land on the ground than to come down the wrong way on the second skateboard.

•• *Barrel jumping*. This is one of the most exciting skateboarding stunts. Like board-to-board jumping, it also involves the use of two boards, plus as many barrels as the skater feels can be safely jumped over. Riding along on one board, the skater approaches the beginning of the line of barrels. On nearing the first barrel, the jumper crouches and then takes off, hoping to land on a second board placed at the end of the line of barrels. Again, do not try to complete your jump if you feel you have started off badly. It is difficult enough to land properly on the second board after you have made a *good* jump. You only increase the risk of injury if you try to make a landing following a poor jump.

•• *High jumping over a bar*. This is one of the most difficult tricks in skateboarding. But, like barrel jumping, it offers the skater and those watching plenty of excitement. What makes this trick so hard to do is that the skater must not only jump high enough to clear the high bar, but must also land upright on the *same* board when coming down. High jumping off a skateboard requires *exact* timing and grace. The skater must make certain that his or her board does not roll too quickly, or too slowly, to the other side of the

By not wearing the proper safety equipment, this young skateboarder makes this a very risky barrel jump.

high bar. Do not attempt this jump without help from an advanced skateboarder.

SLALOM
RIDING

Slalom riding has been a popular form of skiing for many years. Now it is a popular routine among skateboarders who prefer the excitement of speed and continuous movement to tricks and stunts. Slalom skaters ride down a hill or ramp, winding their way around cones or other objects purposely placed there. In contests, the idea is to finish the ride as quickly as possible without knocking down any of the objects.

You needn't concern yourself with speed when you are learning the slalom. Work at your own pace. If no appropriate objects are available, use your imagination to set up a course.

GYMNASTIC
ROUTINES

There is nothing new about people doing headstands, handstands, and other gymnastic tricks. Gymnastics as a sport dates as far back as ancient Greek times. But it was only as recently as the 1970s that these stunts began to be performed with great frequency on skateboards, especially by those who learned gymnastics before they took up skateboarding. Actually, many skating routines are really gymnastic freestyle exercise moves.

Before you rush into trying any of the tricks that follow, you should be aware that even though you may be a good gymnast, you must first learn how to use a skateboard. And even if you are a good skateboarder, you must first learn how to do the gymnastic tricks *off* a skateboard before attempting them *on* the board. Among the most popular skateboard gymnastic tricks are:

•• *Handstand.* A typical skateboard handstand is done by holding one hand on each end of the board. With both feet planted on the board and the body in a crouched position, the skater "pushes off," or gets the board moving. Then he or she lifts their body into a handstand position. If you prefer a faster ride, you could first hold the board above your head and run with it for a few seconds, and then quickly place it on the ground and kick up into the handstand position.

•• *Handplant.* This maneuver requires athletic ability, as well as strength in the upper body. You first do a regular handstand with one hand while, with your other hand, you hold the board atop your feet pointed in a skyward direction. Remain in this position as long as you can, before bringing the board down to the ground. Skateboard gymnasts consider this maneuver to be challenging and exciting. However, anyone wishing to learn this stunt should first perfect the basic handstand.

•• *Ho ho.* Don't let the name fool you. There is nothing funny about the trick to those learning how to do it. A difficult maneuver to learn, a skater per-

forms this stunt by doing a two-hand handstand while balancing the board atop his two feet pointed toward the sky.

To do the maneuver, you first crouch low to the ground as you prepare to perform a one-hand handstand. While in the handstand position, place the skateboard atop your feet with your other hand. Then quickly bring your hand down to the ground to do a two-hand handstand, as you balance the board atop your feet. Remain in the two-handstand position as long as you can continue to balance the board with your feet. To end the stunt, return to the one-handstand position, while removing the board from atop your feet with your other hand. Then you bring the board back down to the ground.

•• *Headstand.* For most skateboarders, learning a headstand is harder than learning a handstand. For one thing, getting your balance is more difficult. You cannot use the strength of your arms, like you can when doing a handstand. Secondly, it is not a comfortable feeling to balance yourself on your head.

One way of doing a headstand is to crouch down low, placing your head toward the front of the board and your knees on the other end. You should look as though you are about to do a forward somersault. With your hands tightly holding the sides of the middle of the board, and with the board in motion, lift yourself slowly up to the headstand position.

The handstand
requires tremendous
upper body strength.

•• *L-and V-sits.* Both these body positions require a *lot* of arm strength. Your hands are placed on the two ends of the board. With the board moving, you lift yourself up, using your hands. The L-sit position involves extending the legs straight out, forming an L-shape with your body. The V-sit position is done by extending the legs slightly upward, creating a V-shape with your entire body.

DOWNHILL
SKATING

Though downhill, or speed, skating is exciting to those who do it, it is also *very* dangerous. The idea is to race down a steep hill as quickly as you can. Most skaters ride in a crouched position, extending their arms straight ahead. The most common stance is to keep both feet planted parallel toward the middle of the board, pointing forward.

Speeds of more than 60 miles (95 km) an hour have been attained by expert speed skaters. But these people are aware that one careless mistake can result in a tragic accident. Downhill skaters must *always* remember to wear a helmet, gloves, knee pads, and elbow pads, in addition to long pants and a long-sleeved shirt. A long, hard deck and thin wheels should also always be used. And you shouldn't even consider speed skating unless you are an advanced skater who has excellent control of your board.

Downhill skating

THE LANGUAGE OF SKATEBOARDING

Skateboarding, like other sports, has developed its own language, its own slang. Some of the terms are more commonly used than others; some are universally popular while others are more popular on a regional rather than national basis. But all contribute to making the skateboard language colorful and exciting. The following are some of the terms you will likely hear when you visit skateboarding areas or watch competitions. A few of them refer to tricks or riding positions not described in the preceding chapter.

Air walks. An exciting and breathtaking stunt, it should only be done by experienced ramp riders. An air walker begins with the maneuver in the judo air position (see judo air), holding the front of the board

Air walking

with one hand, while keeping both feet parallel across the width of the board. As the skater takes off from the ramp, he or she extends one foot forward and the other foot backward, while still holding onto the board. The skater then returns both feet to the board as the maneuver is about to be completed.

Backside move. When a rider turns in the direction of his or her back foot.

Bail. This is something a rider would rather not experience. A skateboarder who is about to bail is one who is about to fall.

Bio. When skateboarders use the term, it does not have anything to do with science. Rather, it is an admiring description of an aerialist who performs excellent high ramp maneuvers.

Blazed. A term used to describe a skateboarder who has ridden exceptionally well.

Christie. Riding with one leg completely bent, the other leg extended to either side or straight ahead. The rider's arms also extend to either side or straight ahead. To do the christie, the skater must have excellent balance.

Coffin. Riding the skateboard flat on your back, with the palms of your hands held together in a praying position under your chin.

Daffy (or *Duck-walk*). Riding with one of your feet placed on the front of one board (causing the back wheels to be lifted off the ground) and the other foot on the rear of a second board (causing the front wheels to be lifted up off the ground). The first board is a short distance in front of the other. The daffy got its name because the skater looks a bit like Daffy Duck, and often acts a bit goofy while riding this way.

These skaters do their variation of the coffin.

Fakie. One of the first maneuvers perfected by vertical wall riders. Riders build up speed so they can ride up a vertical wall and then come back down without turning their boards or bodies. Riders must first perfect this maneuver before attempting more advanced vertical wall, ramp-related activities.

Frontside movement. When a rider turns in the direction of his or her front foot.

Getting air. It has nothing to do with leaving a stuffy room to go outdoors. Rather, it is the momentary point when an aerialist is about to descend the top of a skate-ramp.

Gnarly. An expression often used by skateboarders in complimenting another skater. Expresses the feeling of "Hey, you're really cool. You know how to do it."

Go for it. An expression used by skateboarders when encouraging someone to try a difficult routine. A skateboarder about to "go for it" should remember, however, never to try any stunt or routine that seems too difficult.

Goofy foot. Skating with your left foot across the width of the rear of the board and your right foot across the front of the board. Normally, skaters ride with their left foot in front and their right foot placed in the back.

Hang five. Extending the toes of one foot over the front edge of the board while trying to keep the back wheels from rising off the ground.

Doing the daffy

Hang ten. The same as hang five, except that you use both feet.

Hard core. An expression often used to describe someone who skates in a very aggressive, bold manner.

Hot skateboarding. A term applied to the performance of someone riding his or her board very well.

Judo air. When a skater asks if you are interested in judo, he or she isn't referring to the art of self-defense. Instead, the skater is talking about judo air, an advanced ramp-skating maneuver. While in the air off the top of the ramp, you first get into a crouched position, with both feet resting parallel across the board and one hand holding the edge of the front of the board. As you leave the top of the ramp, extend one foot straight ahead, remaining in that position for a second or two. Then place your foot back onto the board as you complete your ramp ride.

Kickflip. You jump off the board and, at the same time, flip it completely around with your foot. If you succeed, you will be able to land back on top of the board. This stunt is a lot of fun, but it requires perfect timing and a lot of practice.

Lame. When an athlete is described as having "come up lame," it generally means he or she has injured a leg or foot. But when a skateboarder is said to be lame, it simply means he or she is a bad skater.

Madonna. She is certainly an exciting entertainer, but when skateboarders call out "Madonna,"

Frontside air

it's to describe an exciting air maneuver that is about to be performed.

180s. Keeping one foot at one end of the board and the other at the other end, you make quick half-turn movements, keeping the board moving along in one direction.

Poseur. If you dress like a skater and talk like a skater, it does not mean you're a skater. Someone who acts like a skater but doesn't know how to skate is a poseur.

Pulling big hair. When a skater sees another skater soaring through the air, appearing free as a bird, he or she is likely to describe the action as "pulling big hair."

Rock and roll. This doesn't have anything to do with dancing or music. A skater who likes to rock and roll rides his board to the top of a ramp, rocks the board on the ramp's top edge, and makes a turn maneuver before riding the board back to the bottom of the ramp.

Shooting the duck. To do this you ride along slowly with one foot placed on the rear of the board and the other ahead to help you keep your balance. Then you bend deeply, still keeping one foot on the board, the other extended. Slowly, you return to your original position.

Shredding. If a skateboard expert says you are "shredding," you have a right to feel proud. It means you are skating beautifully.

Sketchy. Used to describe someone who skates in an ungraceful, clumsy manner, as though he or she were going to fall or stumble.

Spacewalking. This is similar to kickturns, except that you keep the front of the board off the ground.

Silkscreening a design onto a skateboard can make the board look as wild as some of the stunts.

Stoked. Someone who is very keyed up while skateboarding.

Switch stance. If while the board is in motion, you change from a regular riding stance to a goofy foot stance, you are doing what is called the switch stance.

Traversing. The zigzagging movements used by downhill riders to control their speed.

Tic tac. When a rider presses down on the rear of the board, causing the front wheels to rise off the ground, and then moves forward by swaying the board from left to right on the rear wheels.

Walking the board. This is simply walking forward and backward on your skateboard by crisscrossing your feet while the board is moving.

Walking the dog. If a skateboarder is asked to walk the dog, he or she doesn't start looking for the family pet. Instead, the skater performs the "walk the dog" freestyle maneuver, a popular kickturn-related stunt.

MEET THE SUPERSTARS

TONY
HAWK

When he performs his vertical air magic, there is no one better. His name is Tony Hawk, an aerialist who soars through the air like a high-flying bird, displaying the skills that have earned him the reputation of skateboarding's top star.

A professional since 1982, Hawk has finished first in an overwhelming number of the events that he has entered, winning the national series title competitions sponsored by the National Skateboard Association. No wonder he has been described by more than a few skating colleagues as the Wayne Gretzky of skateboarding, a reference to the superstar hockey player of the National Hockey League.

At six feet (185 cm) and 140 pounds (64 kg), Hawk resembles a cross-country runner more than he does a skateboard aerialist—whose appearance is usually powerful and compact. But when performing his maneuvers, he leaves little doubt that he is a skateboarding marvel. Hawk's routines include exhilarating gymnastic and acrobatic stunts. And just as the world-famous Harlem Globetrotters end their basketball games with exciting flourishes that never fail to bring the crowd to its feet, Hawk holds out his most exciting maneuvers for the very last. An example of his electrifying style of skating is his ability to consistently perform two mid-air somersaults and then complete the maneuver by landing on a small piece of hardwood—the only aerialist in the world capable of performing this stunt.

Hawk was introduced to skateboarding by his older brother, Steve, when he was an eight-year-old Little League baseball player in California. It did not take him long to become totally involved in the sport, practicing at all opportunities. Soon, he was performing maneuvers with such skill and dexterity that it was apparent that he had the makings of a future skateboarding star.

It is very important that if a youngster is to do well in a particular field of activity, he or she receive encouragement from parents and family members. And there was lots of encouragement in Tony Hawk's family. In addition to the advice offered by Steve, Tony's father, Frank, was very active in the sport. The elder Hawk organized the California Amateur Skateboard League (C.A.S.L.) in 1980 and, three years later, organized the National Skateboard Association (N.S.A.). Tony acknowledges that his dad played a very important role in his development as a skateboard superstar and, more importantly, as a person.

In recent years, Tony has appeared in many movie films, videos, and television commercials, which have helped make him the richest skateboarder in the world.

RUSS
HOWELL

When Russ Howell was the best and most famous skateboarder in the world in the 1970s, he served as an ideal role model to young children, often giving free lessons at skating clinics and instructing handicapped youngsters. Since the mid-1980s, Howell has continued to have a positive impact on the lives of children by working as a schoolteacher in the Long Beach, California, area.

Although Howell does not earn the large amount of money he made after becoming the first professional skateboarder in the world, he is very happy with his life. He says that by teaching schoolchildren, he has become rich in spirit. In a letter written on December 21, 1987, Howell said, "I am learning to become richer with less and less money." He added that he is grateful that his status as the original skateboard superstar has provided him with the platform from which to help educate and influence young students.

Known as the granddaddy of skateboarding, Howell originated many of the freestyle stunts and tricks that have been copied and performed by millions of skateboarders throughout the world. Still, Howell continues to compete when he has time to do so, performing superbly. For instance, in 1986, he broke his old record of consecutive spins with a mark of 163 top spins. Howell says he hopes that his record-breaking performance will serve to inspire some older skateboarders to remain active and do well on a competitive basis.

Howell has appeared on many television shows, as well as in movie films and television commercials. Very popular among skateboard fans in Australia, Howell has received widespread recognition for organizing a skateboard curriculum there for high school students.

DIANE
DESIDERIO

Diane Desiderio, the only woman professional skateboard freestylist in the world, has much to overcome when competing against stronger and more aggressive male skaters. But that does not bother Diane. The greater the challenge, the more she enjoys it.

A professional since 1983, Diane acknowledges that it is "very difficult" for a woman to successfully compete against top-ranked male skateboarders. Nevertheless, she has done well, earning the respect and admiration of her male colleagues and competitors. And equally important, she is serving as a role model to many young female skateboard enthusiasts, who might wish to become skateboard pros in the future.

Diane, a resident of San Diego, California, says she basically concentrates on improving her own performance, rather than on finishing ahead of her competitors in an event. In a telephone conversation from her home, she said, "I compete against myself, not against the guys. In the process, I've beaten guys who were real good skaters. It's a great feeling to finish ahead of others but, to me, the greatest feeling is to just go out there and compete. It is very exciting."

As a young teenager in Orange County, California, Diane overcame a more serious challenge than simply competing against male skateboarders. Diane had become heavily involved with drugs and, as a result, became very ill. But through prayer, determination, and the help of loved ones, she overcame her drug problems. Her advice to youngsters is to say "NO" to drugs and to concentrate on constructive, healthy activities.

Diane regularly performs with her husband, Primo, a professional freestyle and streetstyle skateboarder. She has appeared in a number of television commercials and often gives skateboard demonstrations at school functions.

RODNEY
MULLEN

Rodney Mullen is more than just the finest freestyle skater in the world. Mullen, a twenty-one-year-old native of Gainesville, Florida, is an A student at the Florida Institute of Technology and has long been an outstanding role model to the younger skaters and skateboard fans throughout the world.

A perennial world champion freestylist who introduced and popularized the Ollie, Mullen spends a lot of time instructing and chatting with his young fans. Often, youngsters ask Mullen if they can borrow his skateboard for a short while. Rarely does Mullen refuse them. In fact, he usually feels shy about asking a youngster to return the board if his young fan is riding the board for a longer period of time than expected.

A professional skater since the age of thirteen, he won top honors in the Vancouver Expo and the 1988 Chicago Blow Out, among his many other first place finishes. In the Vancouver event, he was the only skater to receive a perfect 100 score. Mullen, who is studying to be a biomedical engineer, is often seen displaying his skating skills on national tours.

TOM
GROHOLSKI

If there is one thing that Tom Groholski enjoys as much as generating his own special brand of ramp-riding excitement, it is talking with youngsters interested in skating. And one of the most important pieces of advice that Tom gives youngsters is to have fun while skateboarding, and not worry about winning or becoming a big star.

One of the top amateur skaters before becoming a pro recently, the North Brunswick, New Jersey, native emphasizes that if skaters try too hard, it could lessen their enjoyment of the sport. Instead of striving to achieve greatness, Tom says youngsters should concentrate on learning how to skateboard properly and on improving their riding skills. The future will take care of itself, Tom believes.

As an expert ramp rider, Tom loves to control his speed and momentum and finds it thrilling to soar through the air performing his aerial maneuvers. But, he emphasizes, inexperienced skateboarders should never attempt ramp-riding stunts.

J. T.
MURPHY

When J. T. Murphy was a college student in the early 1980s, it did not disturb him that he did not own a car or live close to public transportation. He simply traveled 10 miles (16 km) a day to and from school on his skateboard.

One of the top skaters on the East Coast, J. T. has had a love affair with skateboarding. That explains why he often smiles while competing. Murphy says the reason he smiles so often is because he has more fun than most skateboarders.

A director of the Eastern Skateboarding Association, Murphy has finished at the top in many prestigious events. Since 1987, he has been the East Coast streetstyle champion as an unsponsored amateur, the winner of the Brooklyn Bridge streetstyle contest in New York City, and the third-place finisher in an East Coast competition involving choreographed freestyle spins and other maneuvers to music.

When not skating, this resident of Roselle Park, New Jersey, commands equal respect as a professional research scientist in biology. Hard to believe? It shouldn't be, says J. T., who maintains that being a scientist and a top-ranked skateboarder demand an equal amount of dedication and discipline. And, he adds, if a person is willing to make personal sacrifices and work very hard, he or she can achieve any goal.

MICHAEL
KINNEY

Some athletes are particularly graceful, able to perform in an outstanding manner with what appears to be a minimum of effort. One such athlete is Michael Kinney from Spring Lake, New Jersey, who is one of the top young skaters in the United States.

Kinney performs his maneuvers with such grace and precision that many persons have remarked that he does not appear to put much effort into his routines. But experienced skaters know that no one can become as good a skater as Kinney without working very hard. A freestylist since 1985, Kinney attained top honors in 1987, winning the prestigious C.A.S.L. freestyle competition in Anaheim, California, and the Louisiana Get Wet Aggression competition, among other accomplishments.

Although Kinney is expected to be a top skateboarder for many years to come, he has always been aware of the importance of receiving an education. That is why he enrolled at the University of San Diego, where he is doing very well. Kinney hopes ultimately to receive a degree in business administration.

DON
HILLSMAN

Don Hillsman is only 5 feet 2 inches (160 cm) and weighs 120 pounds (54 kg). But don't let his modest physical proportions fool you. His skateboard accomplishments stand tall, and his competitive heart is as big as could be.

One of the most versatile skateboarders in the United States, Hillsman has the rare ability of being able to expertly perform a host of wide-ranging maneuvers. And there aren't many skaters who can do the stunts as well as Hillsman, as evidenced by his having finished at or near the top in virtually every competition he has participated in.

Despite his immense skating accomplishments, this skater from Atlanta, Georgia, is considered by many to be vastly underrated, and whose accomplishments have not been as publicized as those of West Coast skateboarders. But Hillsman is not complaining. He prefers to let his performance speak for itself.

KENNY PAYTON

Kenny Payton was only six-years-old when he received his first skateboard . . . and his second, third, and fourth boards as well. They were all given to him by the father of a young boy who had suffered a serious accident while skateboarding. In the ensuing years, Payton spent almost all his leisure time practicing and enjoying the maneuvers that have made him one of the top vertical wall and ramp skaters.

Payton, who is from Austin, Texas, has won many prominent competitions, including the Benjamin Pro Am ramp contest and the Easy Roller open event in Austin. Even Payton admits he has come a long way since his teenage days when he would hitchhike across the country to compete in skateboarding competitions.

When not skating, Payton can be found surfing in Mexico, snow skiing, announcing skateboard competitions, or judging events. When serving as a judge, Payton is keenly interested in new tricks and maneuvers being performed, in addition to the more familiar routines.

Some other top skateboard stars include Chris Miller, whose unmatched ramp-riding style and skills have earned him a national reputation; Daryll Grogan, a freestylist from Costa Mesa, California, whose parallel handstands, finger tips, and other gymnastic maneuvers are breathtaking; Christian Hosoi, who wows judges and spectators with his ramp aerial maneuvers; Corina Sprieter of Switzerland, the leading woman amateur freestylist; Steve Cabellero, a top vertical rider and freestylist from San Jose, California; Joseph Humeres, a New York City resident and gymnastic routine specialist who was 1987's Eastern freestyle champion; Greg Librizzi, a New Jersey freestylist considered by many as one of the most promising young skaters in the country; Matt "Woody" Wood, who, at the age of fourteen, was already widely recognized for his flawless choreographed routines and is one of the youngest sponsored amateurs in the country; Henry Hester, who draws raves for his slalom and downhill maneuvers; and Jeff Hartsell, a Venice, California, resident known for his extraordinary versatility as a top-ranked skateboarder.

Matt Wood, one of
skateboarding's youngest
and brightest stars

COMPETITIVE
AND PROFESSIONAL
SKATEBOARDING

Although many of the bigger skateboarding contests continue to be held in southern California, where the sport first became popular, prominent events are now commonly held throughout the United States. This has helped create vast interest in the sport in such states as New York, New Jersey, Massachusetts, Maine, Maryland, Missouri, Georgia, Virginia, Florida, Texas, and Arizona.

The creation of the Eastern Skateboarding Association, in late 1986, has been a major factor in the recent growth of the sport in eastern regions of the country. The ESA has organized and sponsored many big events, attracting skaters from all over the United States. Its newsletter has also helped create interest among new skaters and has encouraged parents to volunteer their services to help skateboarding continue its growth. It is not unusual for parents to open

Right: Robert Taylor at the National Skateboarding Association's Southeast Regional Championships. Below: trophy winners at a competition sponsored by the Eastern Skateboarding Association

their homes to skateboarders who have traveled from various parts of the country to compete in events and are in need of overnight accommodations. Whereas skateboard associations were primarily based in California in the 1970s, major associations are now also headquartered in Massachusetts, Arizona, Canada, England, and Australia—all over the United States and the rest of the world.

Most of the bigger competitions consist of a variety of events. All include freestyle and streetstyle competitions. Contests in barrel jumping, high jumping, and 360s are also included sometimes.

In rating the form of skating, the judges take into consideration:

• • How difficult the trick is;
• • How well the skater controls the board;
• • The flow of the routine;
• • The number of tricks done.

Skaters are usually given 90 seconds to complete their routines, which are judged on a point-system basis, using a scale of one through ten. Most maneuvers are now given a rating based on the difficulty of the moves. The more points the skater receives, the better he or she is doing. Skaters can choose any combination of stunts and can even make up their own as they go along.

Those entered in organized contests usually compete against others of the same sex and of about the same age. In the future this may change to allow for people of equal ability to compete against one another..

THE
PROFESSIONALS

An excellent example of how the sport has grown is the dramatic rise in the number of professional skateboarders in the United States and Canada. There were only a few dozen pro riders in the late 1970s, but the figure had risen to more than 120 by 1988. Some of these professional skaters were described in chapter 5. Most professional skaters are sponsored by the manufacturing companies. The skaters make their money mostly by giving demonstrations and exhibitions, lecturing, or acting in skateboarding films and TV commercials. While some pros make more than $100,000 a year, this is still quite low compared to what most top professional athletes in other sports make.

But one day skateboarding may become a popular spectator sport; it is certainly an exciting sport to watch. If it does become a popular spectator sport, there will be lots of opportunities for careers in skateboarding, not only for athletes, but for judges, coaches, and instructors.

THE
SKATEBOARDING
ASSOCIATIONS

If you wish to skateboard in organized competition, you should write to your nearest skateboard association (check the telephone book for your area) or one of those on the following list, to get information. The

As skateboarding continues to grow and become more popular, more fans—spectators and skaters alike—can participate in various aspects of the sport.

association will also keep you informed of skateboard developments in your area if you become a member and may offer membership T-shirts, decals, and discounts at association events. Facing this page is a list of the major skateboard associations in the United States, Canada, England, and Australia.

National Skateboard Association
Sonja Catalano
P.O. Box 3645
San Bernardino, CA 92413
(714) 882-3406

Eastern Skateboarding Association
101 Warren Avenue
Seekonk, MA 02771
(508) 336-4372

California Amateur Skateboard League
(C.A.S.L.)
P.O. Box 30004
San Bernardino, CA 92413

Arizona Amateur Skateboard League
P.O. Box 60664
Phoenix, AZ 85082

Canadian Amateur Skateboard Association
15791 Columbia Avenue
White Rock, British Columbia, Canada
VHB 1L6

English Skateboard Association
Darry Thompson
2, Northcliffe Heights
Kidderminster Works, England

Australian Skateboard Association
John Williams
12-641 Pacific Highway, P.O. Box 2067
Chatswood, Australia

FOR FURTHER READING

Bunting, Glenn. "Skateboards." (How to Make Them—How to Ride Them), Harvey House, 1977.

Davidson, Ben. "The Skateboard Book." Putnam Publisher Group, New York, 1979.

Dickmeyer, Lowell A. "Skateboarding Is for Me." Lerner Publications Co., Minneapolis, Minn., 1978.

Grant, Jack. "Skateboarding." Celestial Arts, Millbrae, California, 1976.

Grubb, Jake. "The Ultimate Skateboard Book." Running Press, Philadelphia, Pa., 1988.

Hawk, Steve. "Skateboard Action." Antioch, Yellow Springs, Ohio, 1988.

"Skateboarding." New American Library (N.A.L.), New York, 1988.

Weir, LaVada. "Skateboards and Skateboarding." Wanderer, New York, 1977.

INDEX